HMH |  (into) **Read**

Writer's Notebook

· ·

GRADE K

Printed in the U.S.A.

ISBN   978-1-328-46053-0

12   0928   27 26 25 24 23 22

4500845329   B C D E F G

Grade
K

Contents

_____ 's

Writer's Notebook

Name _____

Who's That?

A noun can be a word for a person. The word girl is a noun.

✎ Draw two people.

✎ Label your pictures
with nouns.

_____

_ _ _ _ _ _ _ _ _ _ _ _ _ _

_____

Name _____

Plan Your Opinion Piece

Your opinion tells how you think or feel about something.

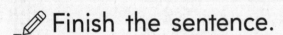 Draw a picture of your favorite book.

 Finish the sentence.

My favorite book is

Name _____

Opinion and Reasons

Your **opinion** tells how you think or feel about something.
A **reason** tells why you feel or think the way you do.

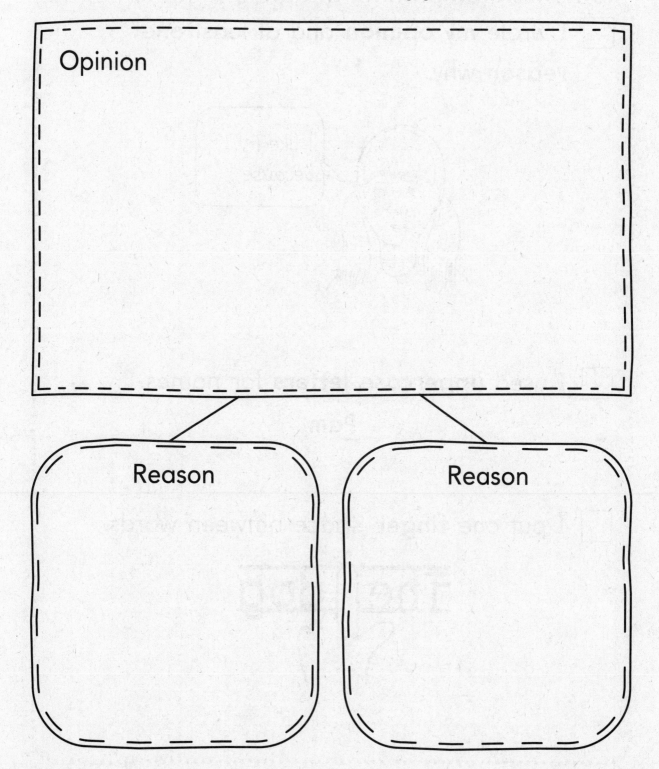

Name _____

Editing Checklist

☑ Read and check your writing.

☐ I wrote my **opinion** and at least one **reason** why.

☐ I used **uppercase letters** for names.

P̲am

☐ I put one **finger space** between words.

10

Name _____

My Topic

A **topic** is what a text is mostly about.

 Draw your topic.

✏️ Write your topic.

_____

- - - - - - - - - - - - - - - - - - -

_____

_____

- - - - - - - - - - - - - - - - - - -

_____

Name _____

We Can!

A verb is an action word. Verbs tell what people do together.

 Trace the action words.

 Draw the action words.

We dance. They clap.

Name _____

Tell Me Why

A reason tells why you feel or think the way you do about something.

✏️ Draw something you like.

✏️ Write one **reason** why you like it.

_____

- -

_____

_____

- -

_____

Name _____

Plan Your Opinion Piece

Your opinion tells how you think or feel about something.

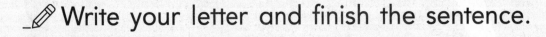 Draw a picture of what you like about school.

 Write your letter and finish the sentence.

My letter is

I like

Name _____

Opinion and Reasons

Your **opinion** tells how you think or feel about something.
A **reason** tells why you feel or think the way you do.

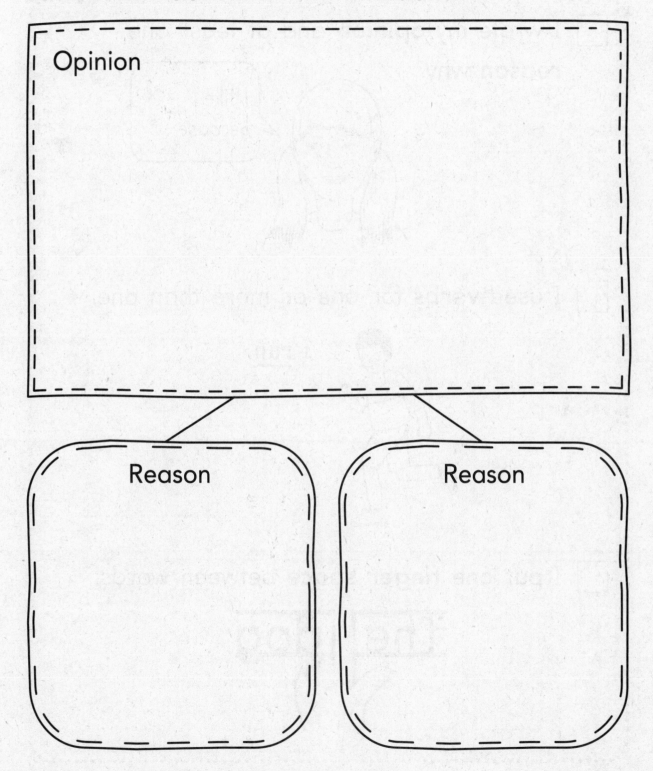

Opinion

Reason

Reason

Name _____

Editing Checklist

☑ Read and check your writing.

☐ I wrote my **opinion** and at least one **reason** why.

☐ I used **verbs** for one or more than one.

I <u>run</u>.

☐ I put one **finger space** between words.

Name _____

Does It Make Sense?

Put the events of a story in an order that makes sense.

👂 Listen to the story events.

✏️ Draw lines to put the events in order.

First

Anton's teacher said hello as he walked in the classroom.

Next

Finally, he put his bag in the closet, ready to start the day!

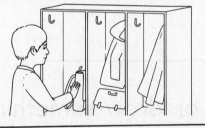

Last

One day, Anton came to school.

Name _____

It's in the Past

A **verb** that ends with **-ed** tells an action that already happened.

✏️ Write **-ed** at the end of the verbs.

1. jump

2. call _____

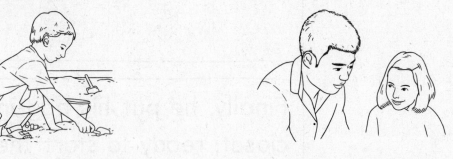

3. play _____   4. talk _____

✏️ Write or draw something you did yesterday.

Name _____

I Told You So!

Verbs can tell about actions that already happened.

✏️ Trace the words.

1. I **eat**.

Yesterday, I __ate__.

2. I **drink**.

Yesterday, I __drank__.

3. I **sleep**.

Yesterday, I __slept__.

✏️ Write a sentence using the word **ran**.

_____
- - - - - - - - - - - - - -
_____
- - - - - - - - - - - - - -
_____

Name _____

Plan Your Story

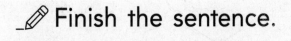 Draw a picture of a new friend. Show where you met the friend.

 Finish the sentence.

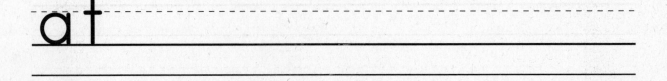

I met _____

at _____

_____

Name _____

Characters and Setting

Characters are the people, animals, or creatures in a story.
The **setting** is where and when a story takes place.

_____

- -

Title: _____

Characters

Setting

Name _____

Editing Checklist

☑ Read and check your writing.

☐ I wrote a story with **characters** and a **setting**.

☐ I used **verbs** to show actions that already happened.

We play_ed_ outside.

☐ I used **uppercase letters**.

W_e saw our friend M_ei.

☐ I put one **finger space** between words.

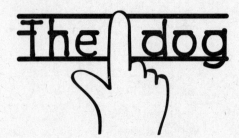

Name _____

Mad, Sad, Glad

Use words that **describe feelings** to add ___ tails to your writing.

✏️ Trace the feeling words.

She is __happy__ to go to school.

He is __sad__ to leave his friends.

We are __scared__ of the dark.

✏️ Write a sentence using a feel_ g word.

_____

- - - - - - - - - - - - - - - - - - -

_____

- - - - - - - - - - - - - - - - - - -

_____

Name _____

Plan Your Story

 Draw a picture of something you learned to do.

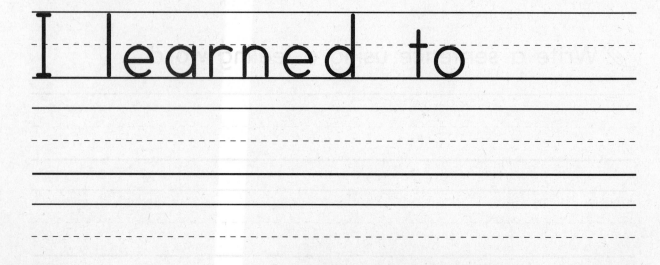 Finish the sentence.

I learned to

Name _____

Characters and Setting

Characters are the people, animals, or creatures in a story.
The **setting** is where and when a story takes place.

_____

- -

Title: _____

Characters

Setting

Name _____

Editing Checklist

☑ Read and check your writing.

☐ I wrote a story with **characters** and a **setting**.

☐ I used **adjectives** and the words **a** and **an** correctly.

She has a (blue) hat.

☐ I used **uppercase letters**.

<u>W</u>e saw our friend <u>M</u>ei.

☐ I put one **finger space** between words.

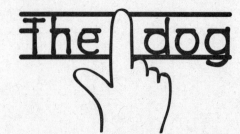

Name _____

It's in the Details

Key details are facts or examples that give more information.

✏️ Draw and write key details about your school.

_____
- - - - - - - - - - - - - - - - -
_____
_____
- - - - - - - - - - - - - - - - -
_____

_____
- - - - - - - - - - - - - - - - -
_____
_____
- - - - - - - - - - - - - - - - -
_____

_____
- - - - - - - - - - - - - - - - -
_____
_____
- - - - - - - - - - - - - - - - -
_____

Name _____

What's That?

A **noun** can be a word for a thing. The word **tree** is a noun.

⭕ Circle the words that are nouns for things.

robot	cat	draw	school
dance	boot	tree	frog

👂 Listen to the riddle.

✏️ Write and draw the noun.

I am red.
I start with the
letter a.
You can eat me for
lunch.

Name _____

Where Am I?

A **noun** can be a word for a place. The word **zoo** is a noun.

⊙ Circle the words that are nouns for places.

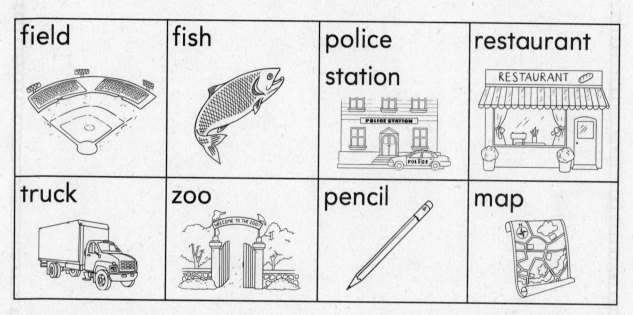

| field | fish | police station | restaurant |
| truck | zoo | pencil | map |

👂 Listen to the riddle.

✏️ Write and draw the noun.

Students learn here.
Teachers work here.
There are many
books here.

Name _____

Plan Your Letter

✏️ Draw a picture of a place in your community.

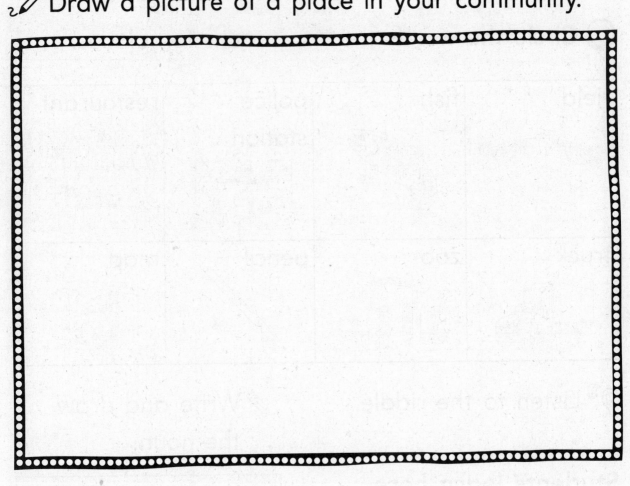

✏️ Finish the sentence.

One place is

36

Name _____

Central Idea and Details

The **central idea** is the most important idea in a text.
Key details give information about the central idea.

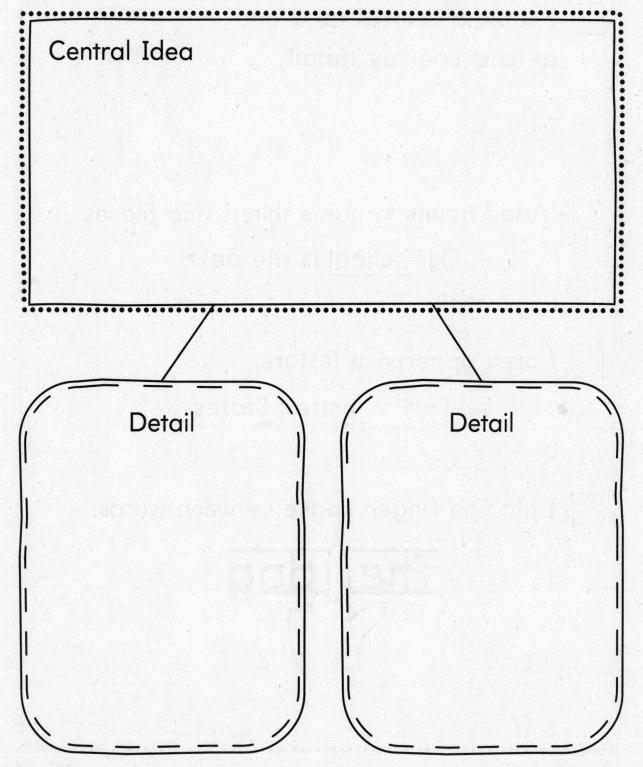

Editing Checklist

☑ Read and check your writing.

☐ I wrote a **central idea** and at least one **key detail**.

☐ I used **nouns** to name things and places.

Our <u>school</u> is the best.

☐ I used **uppercase letters**.

<u>P</u>am   <u>U</u>nited <u>S</u>tates

☐ I put one **finger space** between words.

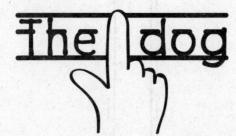

Name _____

List It

Write a **list** to remember things, organize ideas, or share information.

✏️ Write a title for your list.

_____

- -

_____

✏️ Write and draw a list of places you like to go.

1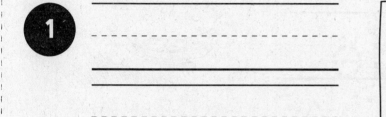

2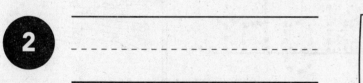

3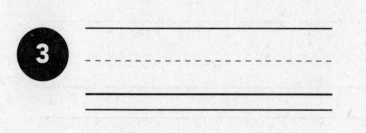

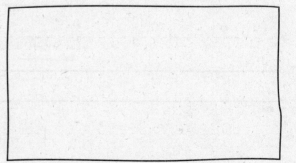

Name _____

So Many Shapes

Use words that **describe shape** to add details to your writing.

✏️ Trace the shape words.

The ball is ___ round ___ .

The lake is ___ wide ___ .

The flagpole is ___ straight ___ .

✏️ Write a sentence using a shape word.

_____

_____

_____

Name _____

Show Your Support

A **key detail** can be an **example** that tells about the **central idea**.

✎ Draw and write examples for the central idea: There are many different ways people get from place to place in our community.

Name _____

How Many?

Use words that describe number to add details to your writing.

✏️ Trace the number words.

I have _____ **two** _____ shoes.

I have _____ **many** _____ friends.

I read _____ **all** _____ the books.

✏️ Write a sentence using a number word.

_____

_____

_____

_____

Name _____

Stick to the Topic

Make sure **key details** tell more about the central idea.

✏️ Cross out the detail that does not fit.

Central Idea

There are many fun activities to do outside in winter.

Detail	Detail	Detail
make a snowman	go sledding	bake cookies

✏️ Write a key detail to add.

_____

_____

_____

_____

Name _____

Plan Your Text

 Draw one way to welcome new neighbors.

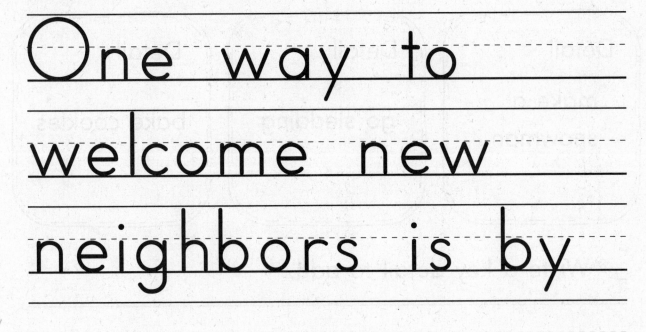 Finish the sentence.

One way to
welcome new
neighbors is by

Name _____

Central Idea and Details

The **central idea** is the most important idea in a text.
Key details give information about the central idea.

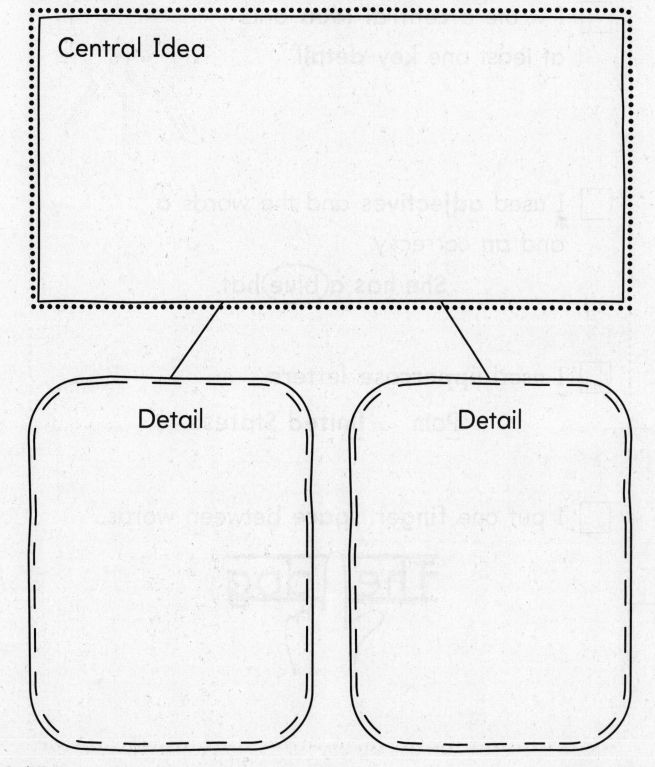

Central Idea

Detail

Detail

Name _____

Editing Checklist

☑ Read and check your writing.

☐ I wrote a **central idea** and at least one **key detail**.

☐ I used **adjectives** and the words **a** and **an** correctly.

She has a(blue)hat.

☐ I used **uppercase letters**.

P̲am   U̲nited S̲tates

☐ I put one **finger space** between words.

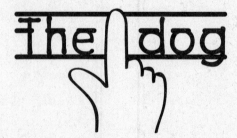

Name _____

The Big Ideas

Start a **noun** that is the name of a person, place, or thing with an **uppercase letter**.

✏️ Color the circle in each group that has a noun that is a name for a person or place.

✏️ Write the names using uppercase letters.

1. (damien) (boy) _____

2. (girl) (maria) _____

3. (ms. wang) (mother) _____

4. (state) (texas) _____

Name _____

Make a Research Plan

Research writing uses sources to answer questions about a topic.

✐ Draw and label one way to exercise.

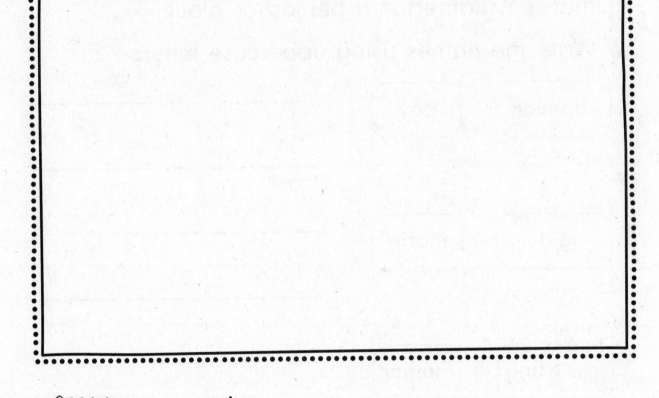

✐ Write a question.

_____

- - - - - - - - - - - - - - - - - - - -

_____

- - - - - - - - - - - - - - - - - - - -

_____

- - - - - - - - - - - - - - - - - - - -

_____

Name _____

Research Map

Use **sources** to write details about your topic.

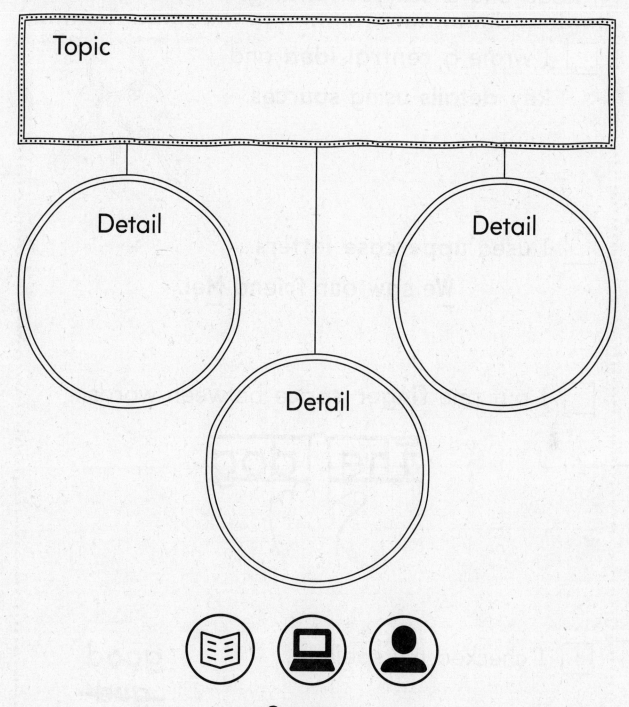

Topic

Detail

Detail

Detail

Sources

🖊 Draw a line to each detail to show your sources.

Editing Checklist

☑ Read and check your writing.

☐ I wrote a **central idea** and **key details** using **sources**.

☐ I used **uppercase letters**.
  We saw our friend Mei.

☐ I put one **finger space** between words.

☐ I checked my **spelling**.

good
~~gud~~

Name _____

Find It in a Book

A book can be a **source** to learn more about your topic.

✏️ Write your topic.

_____

- -

_____

✏️ Draw and label a picture of your source.

Name _____

To the Point

A **period** is a mark at the end of a telling sentence.

◯ Circle the periods.

1. I like to jump up and down.

2. We went to the park today.

✏ Write the missing periods.

3. She went down the slide

4. He hopped over the box

✏ Write a telling sentence. Start with an uppercase letter. Put a period at the end.

_____

- - - - - - - - - - - - - - -

_____

_____

- - - - - - - - - - - - - - -

_____

Name _____

Talk to Experts

An expert can be a **source** to learn more about your topic.

✎ Draw people who are experts on your topic.

✎ Label the experts in your picture.

All Finished

A **sentence** is a complete thought. A sentence starts with an **uppercase letter** and ends with a **period** or other end mark.

✏️ Write the parts of a sentence.

person or thing	action word	end mark

✏️ Draw a picture of your sentence.

✏️ Write your sentence.

_____

- -

_____

Name _____

Find It Online

Find sources online to learn more about your topic.

Draw a picture of something you want to learn more about.

Write words you can use to search online.

Name _____

Make a Research Plan

Research writing uses sources to answer questions about a topic.

 Draw and label one way sleep helps people.

 Write a question.

_____

_____

_____

_____

Name _____

Research Map

Use **sources** to write details about your topic.

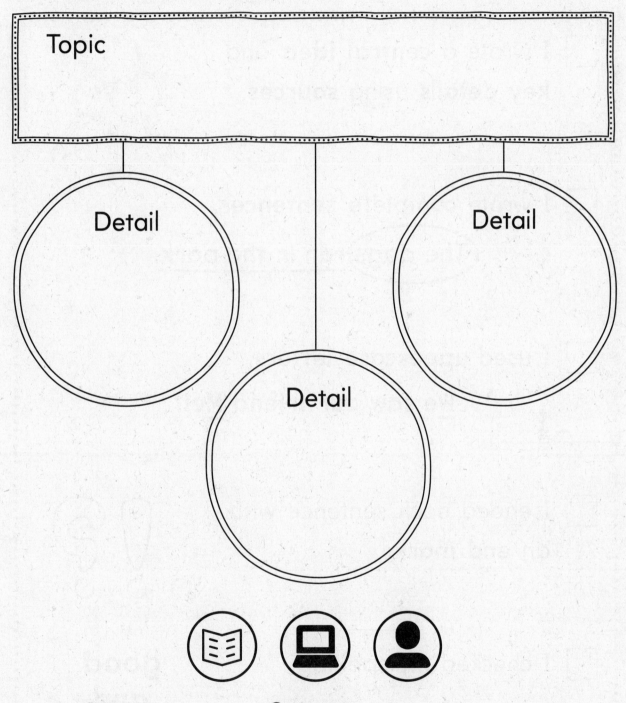

Topic

Detail

Detail

Detail

Sources

✏️ Draw a line to each detail to show your sources.

Name _____

Editing Checklist

☑ Read and check your writing.

☐ I wrote a **central idea** and **key details** using **sources**.

☐ I wrote **complete sentences**.

The dogs ran in the park.

☐ I used **uppercase letters**.

We saw our friend Mei.

☐ I ended each sentence with an **end mark**.

☐ I checked my **spelling**.

good
~~gud~~

Name _____

Story Map

_____

Title: _____

Beginning

Middle

End

Name _____

Editing Checklist

☑ Read and check your writing.

☐ I wrote a **beginning**, **middle**, and **end**.

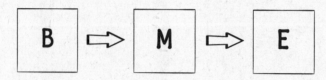

☐ I used **I**, **me**, and **we** correctly.

Sam helped (me).

☐ I used **uppercase letters**.

We saw our friend Mei.

☐ I ended each sentence with an **end mark**.

☐ I checked my **spelling**.

good
~~gud~~

Name _____

First Things First

A strong beginning gets the reader's attention.

✎ Draw and write a topic for a story.

○ Circle one way to start the story.

sound   **dialogue**   **single word**

✎ Write a strong beginning.

_____

- - - - - - - - - - - - - - - - - - -

_____

- - - - - - - - - - - - - - - - - - -

_____

Name _____

One, Two, Three

Nouns that name more than one thing usually end in **–s**.

 Use a paper clip to spin.

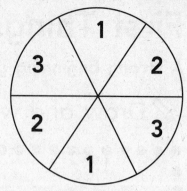

✏ Write the number.	⭕ Circle the word.	✏ Draw a picture.
	cat cats	
	jet jets	
	bed beds	
	rug rugs	

Name _____

And Then . . .

Stories usually tell about events in the order they happened.

👂 Listen to the story.

> First, Kali and her mom went to buy food at the store. Next, Kali helped wash the fruits and vegetables. In the end, they had a yummy dinner.

✏️ Write 1, 2, or 3 to put the events in order.

Name _____

s Wants to Join!

📖 Read each sentence.

✏️ Write the word that means more than one of the <u>underlined</u> word.

_____

- - - - - - - - - - - - - - - -

1. Meg fed the <u>hen</u>.   _____

_____

- - - - - - - - - - - - - - - -

2. Dad had my <u>pen</u>.   _____

_____

- - - - - - - - - - - - - - - -

3. Ben sat on the <u>bed</u>.   _____

✏️ Write a sentence with a noun that means more than one thing.

_____

- - - - - - - - - - - - - - - -

_____

_____

- - - - - - - - - - - - - - - -

_____

Name _____

Link Up!

Use signal words to put story events in order.

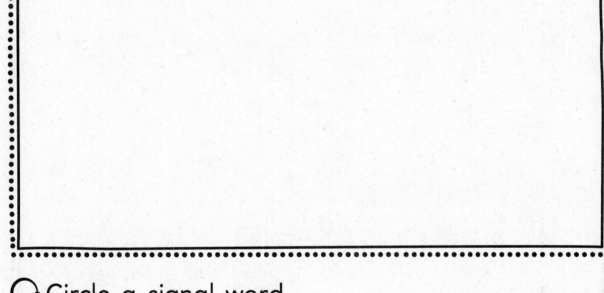 Draw an event from a story.

⭕ Circle a signal word.

After	Later	Then
Finally	Until	Next

✏️ Use the signal word to write what happens next.

_____

_____

_____

Name _____

Plan Your Story

 Draw a picture of a time you did not quit.

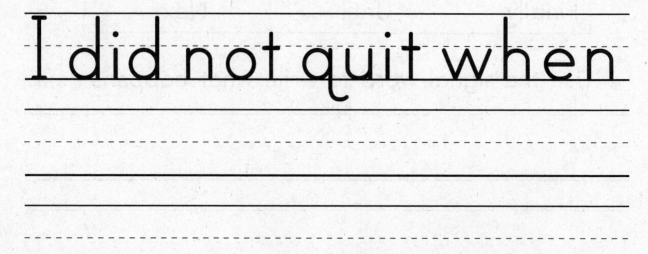 Finish the sentence.

I did not quit when

Name _____

Story Map

_____

- -

Title: _____

Beginning

Middle

End

Name _____

Editing Checklist

☑ Read and check your writing.

☐ I wrote a **beginning**, **middle**, and **end**.

$$\boxed{B} \Rightarrow \boxed{M} \Rightarrow \boxed{E}$$

☐ I used **nouns to show one or more than one** correctly.

dog   dog<u>s</u>

☐ I used **uppercase letters**.

<u>W</u>e saw our friend <u>M</u>ei.

☐ I ended each sentence with an **end mark**.

☐ I checked my **spelling**.

good
~~gud~~

Name _____

Is It Important?

Write all of the **important information** in the steps of a how-to text.

✏️ Draw and write the missing step.

How to Make Popcorn

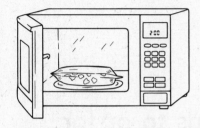

1. Put the popcorn bag right-side up in the microwave.

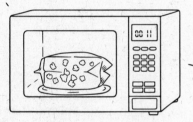

2. Start the microwave to pop the popcorn.

3. _____
   _____
   _____

4. Pour the popcorn in a bowl, and enjoy!

Name _____

Where to? What for?

Use the words **to** and **for** to link nouns to other words.

⭕ Circle the words **to** and **for**.

1. Jocelyn came **to** my house.

2. My brother runs **for** exercise.

✏️ Finish the sentences with the words **to** or **for**.

3. The gift is _____ my friend.

4. Erik went _____ the movie theater.

✏️ Write a sentence using **to** or **for**.

_____

_____

_____

Name _____

Let's Connect

Use the words **from**, **of**, and **with** to link nouns to other words.

⭕ Circle the words **from**, **of**, and **with**.

1. The bus comes **from** the city.

2. Pass me three **of** those books.

3. Lily sits at the table **with** me.

✏️ Finish each sentence with **from**, **of**, or **with**.

4. I make pancakes _____ my dad.

5. We get eggs _____ the market.

6. My sister and I eat all _____ them!

✏️ Write a sentence using **from**, **of**, or **with**.

_____

_____

_____

_____

Name _____

Plan Your How-To Book

✏️ Draw a picture of your favorite game.

✏️ Finish the sentence.

My favorite

game is

Name _____

Organize a How-To Book

How-to books teach readers how to do or make something.

_____
- - - - - - - - - - - - - - - - -

How to _____

_____
- - - - - - - - - - - - - - - - -
_____
_____
- - - - - - - - - - - - - - - - -
_____

_____
- - - - - - - - - - - - - - - - -
_____
_____
- - - - - - - - - - - - - - - - -
_____

_____
- - - - - - - - - - - - - - - - -
_____
_____
- - - - - - - - - - - - - - - - -
_____

79

Name _____

Editing Checklist

☑ Read and check your writing.

☐ I wrote the **important information** and put the **steps in order**.

☐ I used the words **for**, **to**, **from**, **of**, and **with** correctly.

> We went (to) the park.

☐ I used **uppercase letters**.

> We saw our friend Mei.

☐ I ended each sentence with an **end mark**.

☐ I checked my **spelling**.

> good
> ~~gud~~

Start Strong

A **strong beginning** gets the reader's attention.

 Draw and label a picture of your topic.

○ Circle one way to start the text.

question   **interesting fact**   **single word**

✏ Write a strong beginning.

_____

- -

_____

_____

- -

_____

81

Name _____

Who's He? Who's She?

Use the words **he** or **she** to tell about another person.

📖 Read each sentence.　○ Circle the right word.

1. **He / She** likes
to swing with his friends.

2. **He / She** eats
her snack at recess.

3. **He / She** feeds
his dog in the morning.

✏️ Write a sentence with **he** or **she**.

_____

- - - - - - - - - - - - - - -

_____

- - - - - - - - - - - - - - -

_____

Is It Important?

Write key details that tell readers **important information.**

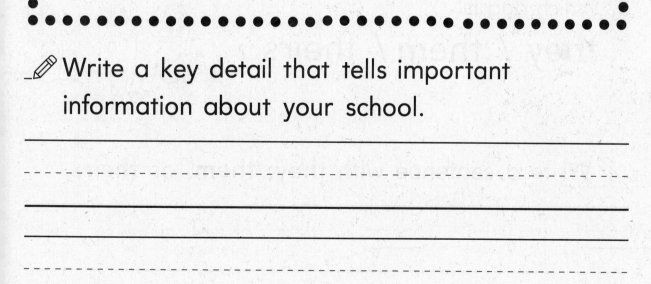 Draw a picture of your school.

_✎ Write a key detail that tells important
information about your school.

_____

- -

_____

- -

_____

- -

_____

Name _____

Who Are They?

Use the words **they**, **them**, or **theirs** to tell about two or more people.

📖 Read each sentence. ⭕ Circle the right word.

1. # They / Them / Theirs
play outside.

2. The house belongs to
they / them / theirs.

3. Which dog is
they / them / theirs ?

✏️ Write a sentence with **they**, **them**, or **theirs**.

_____

- -

_____

- -

_____

Make Every Word Count

Think about the words you use and choose **strong words**.

👂 Listen to the sentences.

⭕ Circle the strong word choice.

1. Our teacher read a

   # good / wonderful

   book.

2. Whales are

   # enormous / big

   animals.

3. She **dashed / ran**

   after the ball.

4. We are

   # happy / excited

   to celebrate the holiday.

85   Module 6 • Week 3

Name _____

Plan Your Text

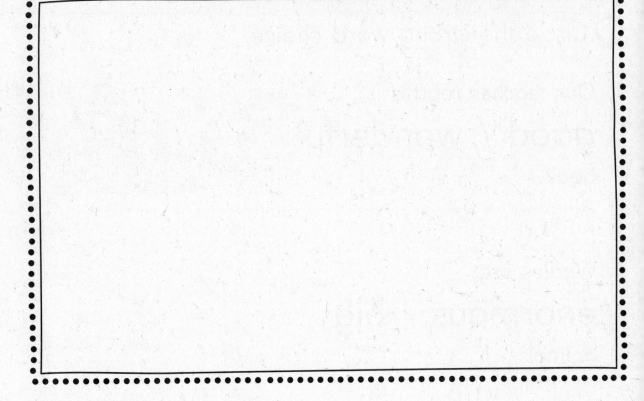 Draw a picture of a holiday you celebrate.

✎ Finish the sentence.

One holiday I

celebrate is

Name _____

Central Idea and Details

The **central idea** is the most important idea in a text.
Key details give information about the central idea.

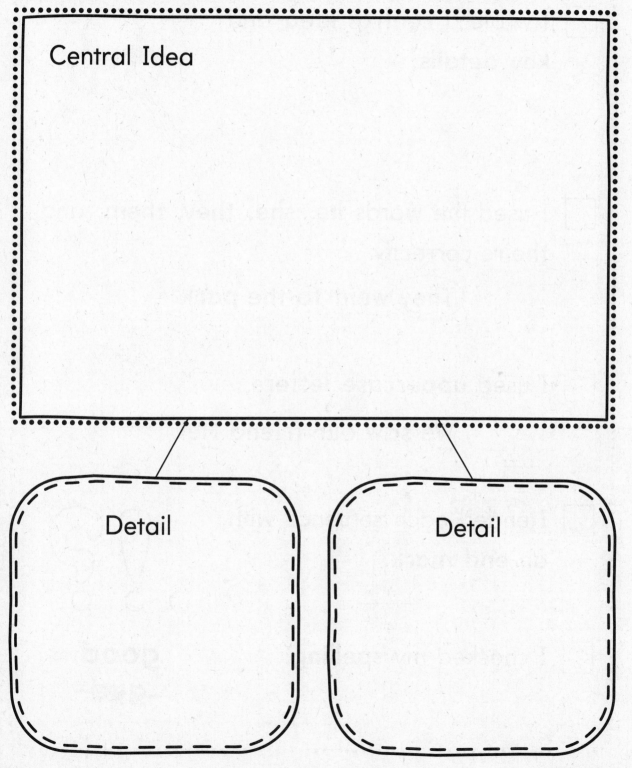

Central Idea

Detail

Detail

Name _____

Editing Checklist

☑ Read and check your writing.

☐ I wrote a **central idea** and **key details**.

☐ I used the words **he, she, they, them,** and **theirs** correctly.

(They) went to the park.

☐ I used **uppercase letters**.

We saw our friend Mei.

☐ I ended each sentence with an **end mark**.

☐ I checked my **spelling**.

good
~~gud~~

Name _____

Use Your Senses!

Sensory words describe what you taste, see, feel, hear, and smell.

✏️ Draw lines to connect the sensory words to the sense or senses they describe.

sweet

pretty

soft

buzz

bitter

crooked

salty

bumpy

burnt

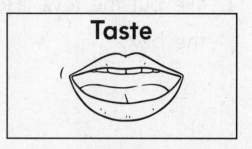
Taste

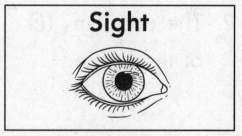
Sight

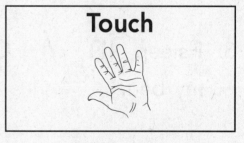
Touch

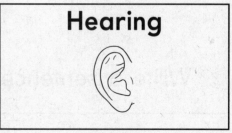
Hearing

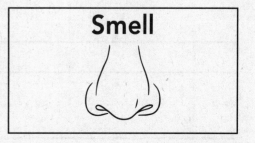
Smell

Name _____

Are You In or Out?

Use the words in and out to tell where something is.

📖 Read each sentence. ⭕ Circle the right word.

1. We put the toys in / out
   the box.

2. The dog ran in / out
   of the house.

3. I sleep in / out
   my bed.

✏️ Write a sentence that uses **in** or **out**.

_____
- -
_____
- -

Name _____

Right On!

Use the words on, off, and by to tell where something is.

✏️ Write a word from the box in each sentence.

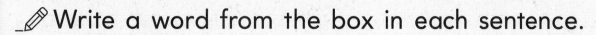

off	**by**	**on**

_____
- - - - - - - - - -

1. I poured syrup _____ the pancakes.

_____
- - - - - - - - - -

2. She took the book _____ the shelf.

_____
- - - - - - - - - -

3. The car drove _____ my house.

✏️ Write a sentence that uses **on**, **off**, or **by**.

_____

- -

_____

- -

_____

91

Plan Your Story

 Draw a picture of an animal and setting.

 Finish the sentences.

My animal is

My setting is

Name _____

Story Map

_____
- -

Title: _____

Beginning

Middle

End

Editing Checklist

☑ Read and check your writing.

☐ I wrote a **beginning**, **middle**, and **end**.

B ⇒ M ⇒ E

☐ I used the words **in, out, on, off,** and **by** correctly.

The cat is (in) the box.

☐ I used **uppercase letters**.

We saw our friend Mei.

☐ I ended each sentence with an **end mark**.

☐ I checked my **spelling**.

good
~~gud~~

Name _____

Line Up!

An **acrostic poem** spells out a topic with one letter on each line.

✏️ Write one letter of your name in each box.

✏️ Draw a picture of yourself. Add details.

Say It with Feeling!

An **exclamation mark** is an end mark that shows strong feelings.

👂 Listen to each sentence.

✏ Write a period or exclamation mark.

_____
- - - - - - - -

1. You did a great job _____

_____
- - - - - - - -

2. I feel like going home _____

_____
- - - - - - - -

3. That play was amazing _____

_____
- - - - - - - -

4. Please clean your room _____

_____
- - - - - - - -

5. Watch out for the car _____

_____
- - - - - - - -

6. I'm so scared of that movie _____

Name _____

Write an Acrostic Poem

An acrostic poem spells out a topic with one letter on each line.

✏️ Write one letter of your name in each box.

✏️ Write a describing word for each letter.

Name _____

Plan Your Poem

 Draw and write the topic for your poem.

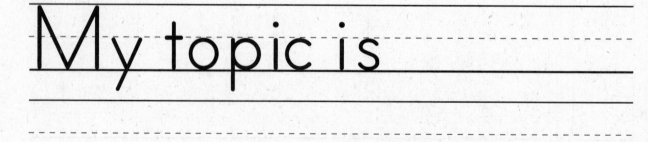 Finish the sentence.

My topic is _____

_____

_____

Five Senses Map

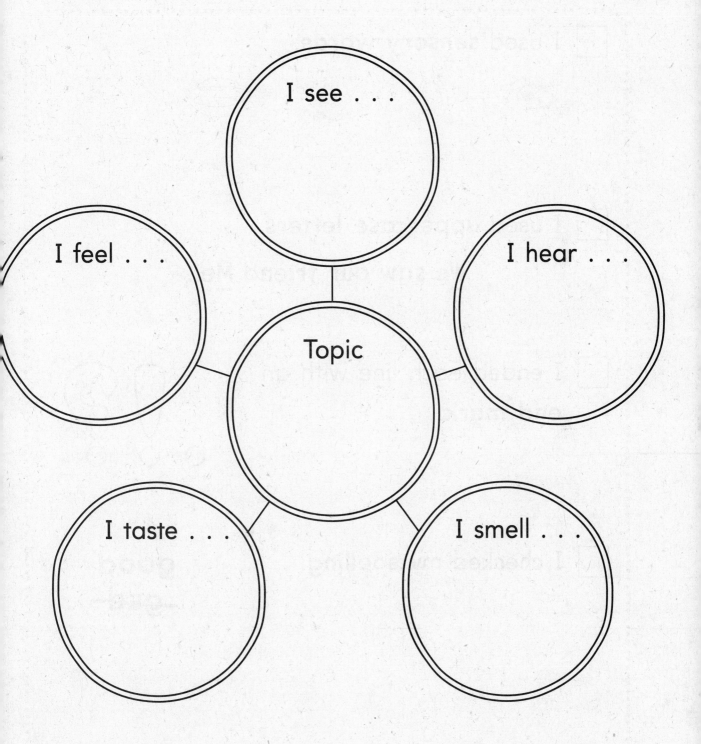

Name _____

Editing Checklist

☑ Read and check your writing.

☐ I used **sensory words**.

☐ I used **uppercase letters**.

<u>W</u>e saw our friend <u>M</u>ei.

☐ I ended each line with an **end mark**.

☐ I checked my **spelling**.

good
~~gud~~

Fact or Opinion?

Opinions are what someone feels or thinks about something.
Facts give information that is true.

🖉 Circle **O** if the sentence is an opinion or **F** if
the sentence is a fact.

1. I think pink is the best color.   O   F

2. Cheetahs run fast.   O   F

3. I like pears.   O   F

4. The sky is blue.   O   F

5. Soccer is the best sport.   O   F

6. Math is my favorite part of the day.   O   F

🖉 Write an opinion.

_____

_____

_____

Name _____

Is It Complete?

A **sentence** is a complete thought. A sentence starts with an uppercase letter and ends with an end mark.

✐ Color the check mark next to each complete sentence.

1. We play in the park.

2. a small red car

3. My dad runs fast.

4. made lunch for school

5. ate at a restaurant

6. William paints at school.

Name _____

Let's Fix It!

A **sentence** is a complete thought. A sentence starts with an uppercase letter and ends with an end mark.

👂 Listen to the incomplete sentence.

The happy child in the park.

✏️ Write the parts to make a complete sentence.

	Describing word	Who or what?	Does what?	Where?
The				

✏️ Write the complete sentence.

_____

- - - - - - - - - - - - - - - - - -

_____

- - - - - - - - - - - - - - - - - -

_____

- - - - - - - - - - - - - - - - - -

_____

Name _____

Plan Your Opinion

Your **opinion** tells how you think or feel about something.

 Draw the most important animal in a garden.

 Finish the sentence.

I think _____

_____ are

most important.

Name _____

Opinion and Reasons

Your **opinion** tells how you think or feel about something.
A **reason** tells why you feel or think the way you do.

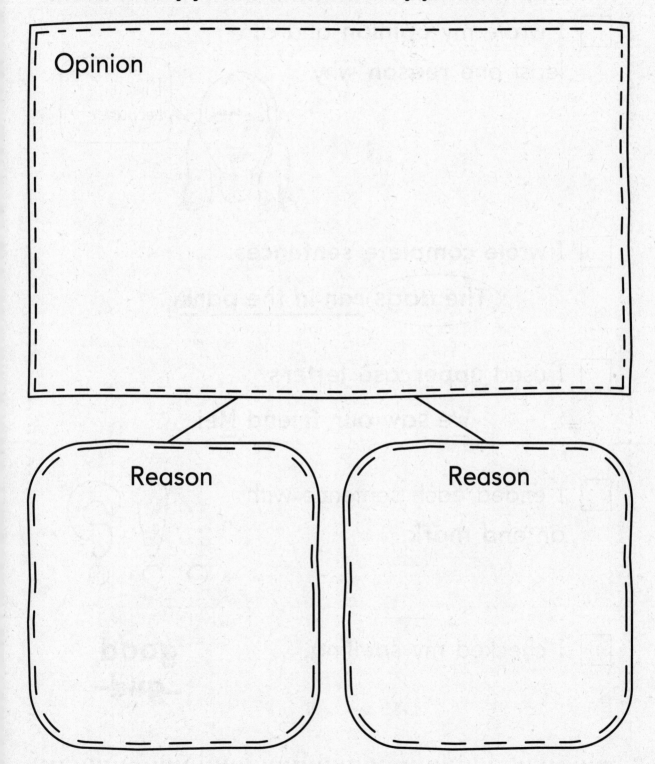

Opinion

Reason   Reason

Name _____

Editing Checklist

☑ Read and check your writing.

☐ I wrote my **opinion** and at least one **reason** why.

I like . . . because . . .

☐ I wrote **complete sentences**.

The dogs ran in the park.

☐ I used **uppercase letters**.

We saw our friend Mei.

☐ I ended each sentence with an **end mark**.

☐ I checked my **spelling**.

good
~~gud~~

What Do You Think?

Write your opinion first. Then write reasons to tell why.

✏️ Write a **1** in the box to put each **opinion** first.

✏️ Write a **2** next to each **reason**.

☐ I like school.

☐ We play games at school.

☐ I think recess should be longer.

☐ We would have more time to play soccer.

☐ I can play with friends.

☐ My favorite game is tag.

Now and Later

The word **will** plus a **verb** tells an action that will happen later.

✏️ Write the verbs to complete each sentence.

read

_____

- -

1. Ava _____ the book later.

write

_____

- -

2. She _____ the letter tomorrow.

plant

_____

- -

3. Jay _____ a tree next year.

✏️ Write about something you will do tomorrow.

_____

- -

_____

- -

_____

Name _____

Give Me a Reason

Good writers add reasons to make their opinions stronger.

 Draw your **opinion**: What is the best pet?

 Write two **reasons** for your **opinion**.

_____

- - - - - - - - - - - - - - - - - - -

1. _____

_____

- - - - - - - - - - - - - - - - - - -

_____

- - - - - - - - - - - - - - - - - - -

2. _____

_____

- - - - - - - - - - - - - - - - - - -

_____

Name _____

Now or Then?

Verbs can tell what is happening now or what happens always.
Verbs can also tell what already happened.

📖 Read each sentence. ⭕ Circle the correct verb.

1. She (looks / looked) for you yesterday.

2. They (walk / walked) home every day.

3. He always (cooks / cooked) dinner.

4. We (play / played) tag last week.

✏️ Write about something that always happens.

_____

_____

_____

✏️ Write about something that already happened.

_____

_____

_____

Name _____

End It Right

A **strong ending** can change minds or make something happen.

✏ Write your opinion.

_____
- -
_____
- -
_____
- -
_____

◯ Circle one way to end the opinion piece.

repeat opinion   strong feeling   call to action

✏ Write a strong ending.

_____
- -
_____
- -
_____
- -
_____

Name _____

Plan Your Opinion Piece

Your opinion tells how you think or feel about something.

✏️ Draw what you would like to grow in a garden.

✏️ Finish the sentence.

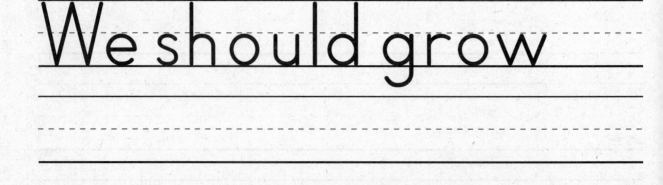

We should grow

Name _____

Opinion and Reasons

Your **opinion** tells how you think or feel about something.
A **reason** tells why you feel or think the way you do.

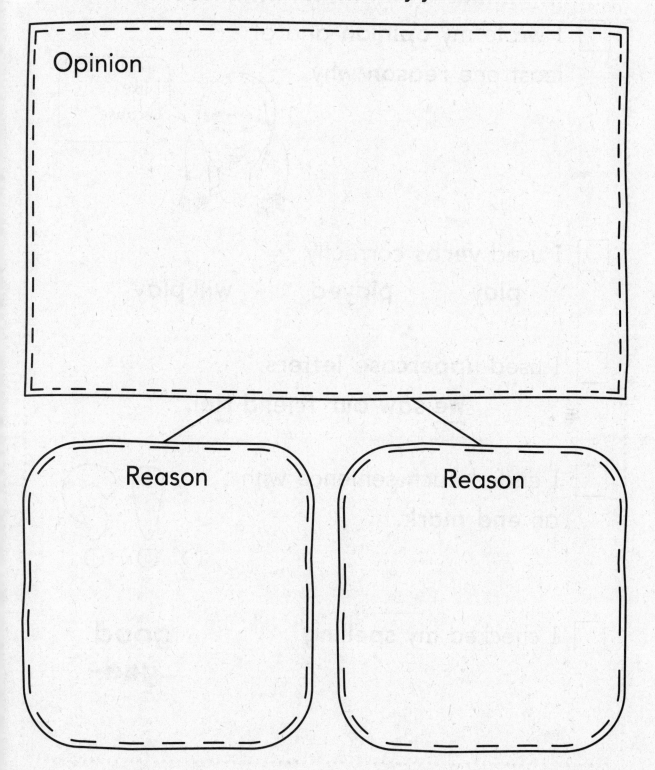

113

Name _____

Editing Checklist

☑ Read and check your writing.

☐ I wrote my **opinion** and at least one **reason** why.

I like . . .
because . . .

☐ I used **verbs** correctly.

play   played   will play

☐ I used **uppercase letters**.

We saw our friend Mei.

☐ I ended each sentence with an **end mark**.

☐ I checked my **spelling**.

good
~~gud~~

Go to the Source

Use **sources** to find information about a topic.

✏️ Draw and write a topic you want to research.

Topic

✏️ Draw and write ideas for sources.

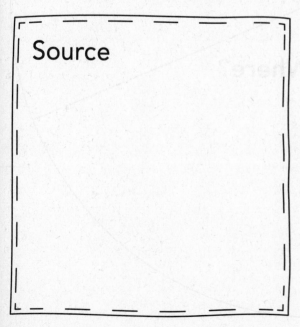

Source

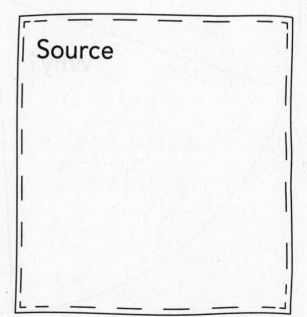

Source

Name _____

The Five Ws

Ask **questions** to learn more about a research topic.

✏ Write a topic and questions you have about it.

_____

- -

Topic: _____

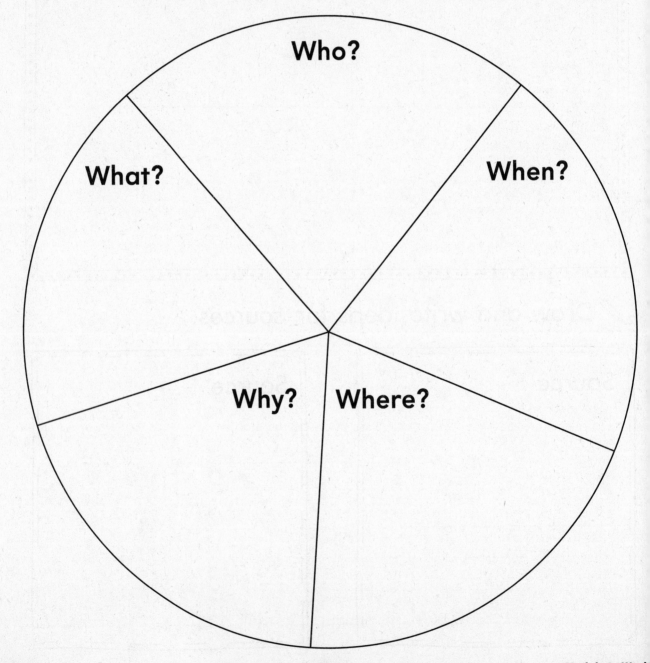

Name _____

Any Questions?

A **question mark** is a mark at the end of an asking sentence.

◯ Circle the question words.

✎ Draw a line under the question marks.

Where do you go to school?

When does school start?

✎ Write the question words and question marks.

_____   _____
- - - - - - - - - - - - - - - - - - -   - - - - - -

_____ is for lunch _____
_____   _____
- - - - - - - - - - - - - - - - - - -   - - - - - -

_____ is your teacher _____

✎ Write an asking sentence. Start with an
   uppercase letter. Put a question mark at the end.

_____
- -

_____

_____
- -

_____

117

Name _____

Make a Research Plan

✏️ Draw and label a picture of a wild animal.

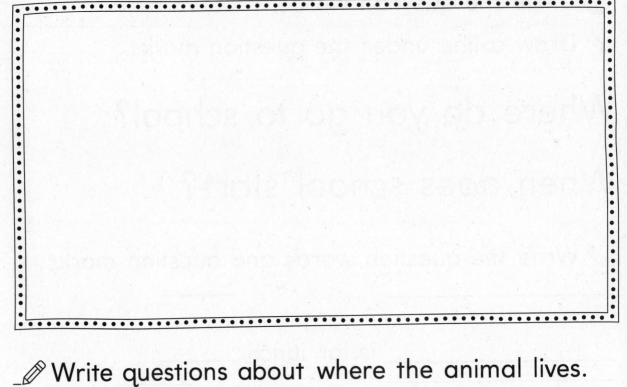

✏️ Write questions about where the animal lives.

_____

- -

_____

- -

_____

- -

_____

- -

_____

Name _____

Research Map

Use **sources** to write details about your topic.

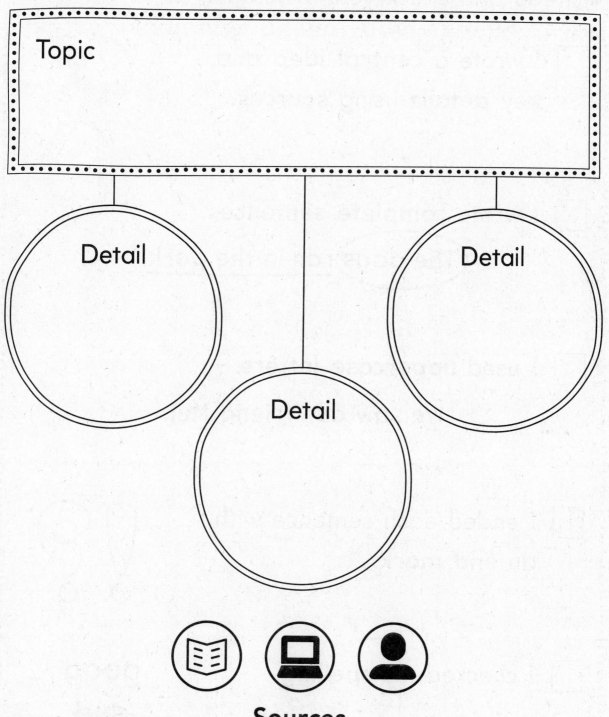

Topic

Detail

Detail

Detail

Sources

✏️ Draw a line to each detail to show your sources.

Name _____

Editing Checklist

☑ Read and check your writing.

☐ I wrote a **central idea** and **key details** using **sources**.

☐ I wrote **complete** **sentences**.

(The dogs) ran in the park.

☐ I used **uppercase letters**.

<u>W</u>e saw our friend <u>M</u>ei.

☐ I ended each sentence with an **end mark**.

☐ I checked my **spelling**.

good
~~gud~~

Name _____

Go Online

You can ask a question to search for information online.

 Draw a topic you want to learn more about.

✏ Write a question you can use to search online.

_____

- - - - - - - - - - - - - - - - - -

_____

_____

- - - - - - - - - - - - - - - - - -

_____

_____

- - - - - - - - - - - - - - - - - -

_____

Name _____

Search Out Sources

Use different **sources** to find information about a topic.

✏️ Draw and write a topic you want to research.

✏️ Draw and write ideas for sources.

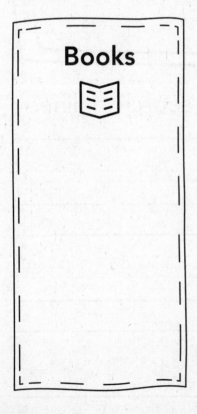

Books

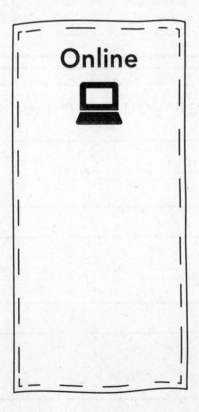

Online

Experts

Name _____

End Strong

A **strong ending** can help readers remember your writing.

✏️ Write the topic.

_____

- -

_____

- -

_____

- -

_____

⭕ Circle one way to end the research report.

conclusion   question   call to learn more

✏️ Write a strong ending.

_____

- -

_____

- -

_____

- -

_____

Name _____

Tell. Ask? Exclaim!

An **end mark** is like a stop sign at the end of a sentence.
End marks tell readers how to read your writing.

📖 Read each sentence.

✏️ Write the missing end marks.

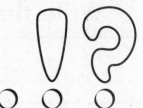

What do dogs eat ____

Dogs have four legs ____

I love dogs ____

✏️ Write a telling, asking, or exciting sentence.
   Use the correct end mark.

_____

_____

_____

_____

Name _____

Show It

Use a **diagram** with **labels** to show new information or help readers understand something better.

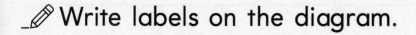 Draw a diagram of an animal's habitat.

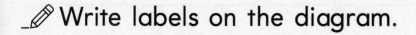 Write labels on the diagram.

Name _____

Make a Research Plan

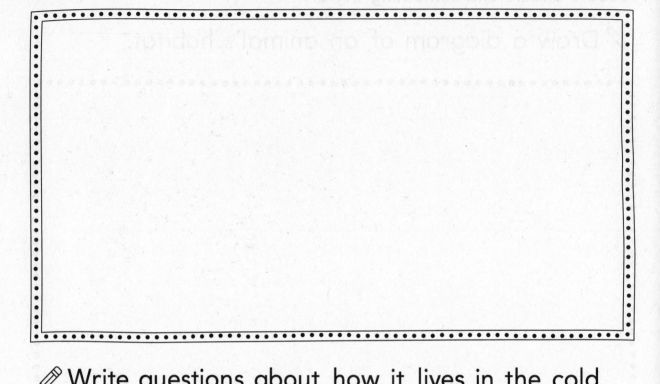

Draw and label a picture of a polar animal.

Write questions about how it lives in the cold.

_____

- - - - - - - - - - - - - - - - - - -

_____

_____

- - - - - - - - - - - - - - - - - - -

_____

_____

- - - - - - - - - - - - - - - - - - -

_____

Name _____

Research Map

Use **sources** to write details about your topic.

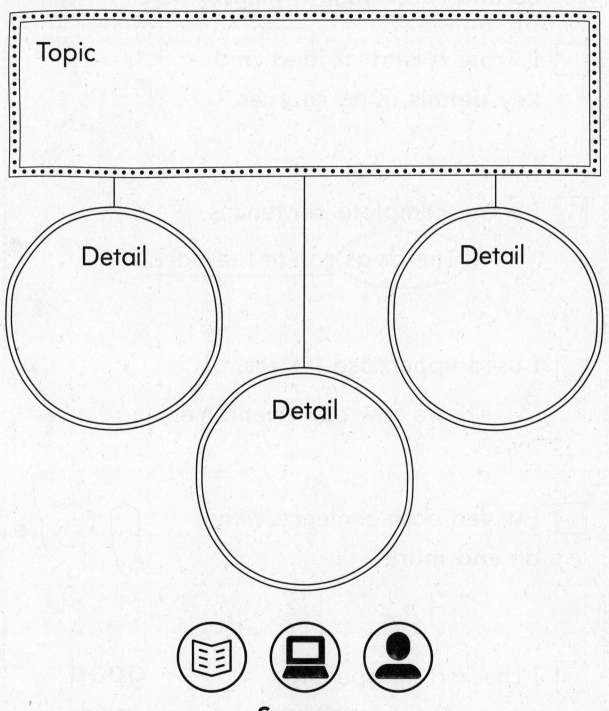

Topic

Detail

Detail

Detail

Sources

✏️ Draw a line to each detail to show your sources.

Name _____

Editing Checklist

☑ Read and check your writing.

☐ I wrote a **central idea** and
key details using **sources**.

☐ I wrote **complete sentences**.

(The dogs)ran in the park.

☐ I used **uppercase letters**.

We saw our friend Mei.

☐ I ended each sentence with
an **end mark**.

☐ I checked my **spelling**.

good

~~gud~~

My Writing Guide

Name _____

Opinion Writing

An **opinion** tells what you feel
or think about something

I think

I like

My favorite _____
is _____.

and the **reasons** why you
feel or think the way you do.

My favorite color
is **yellow** <u>because
I like bananas.</u>

Name _____

STORY WRITING

has <u>characters</u>

has a <u>setting</u>

Beginning
 GO

| First... | One day... |

Middle
 ACTION

| Then... | Next... |

End
 STOP

| Last... | In the end... |

Name _____

Writing to Teach

An <u>informational text</u> is writing that teaches about a topic.

page 118

Name _____

Central Idea and Key Details

topic
what a text is about in one or two words

central idea
the most important idea in a text

key details
facts or examples that give information about the central idea

Keys

Keys open doors.

This key opens the front door.

This key opens the garage door.

This key opens a secret door!

Name _____

Research Writing

If you want to know more about a topic, do **research**!

Use **sources** to find information.

Read a book.

Look online.

Ask an expert.

Name _____

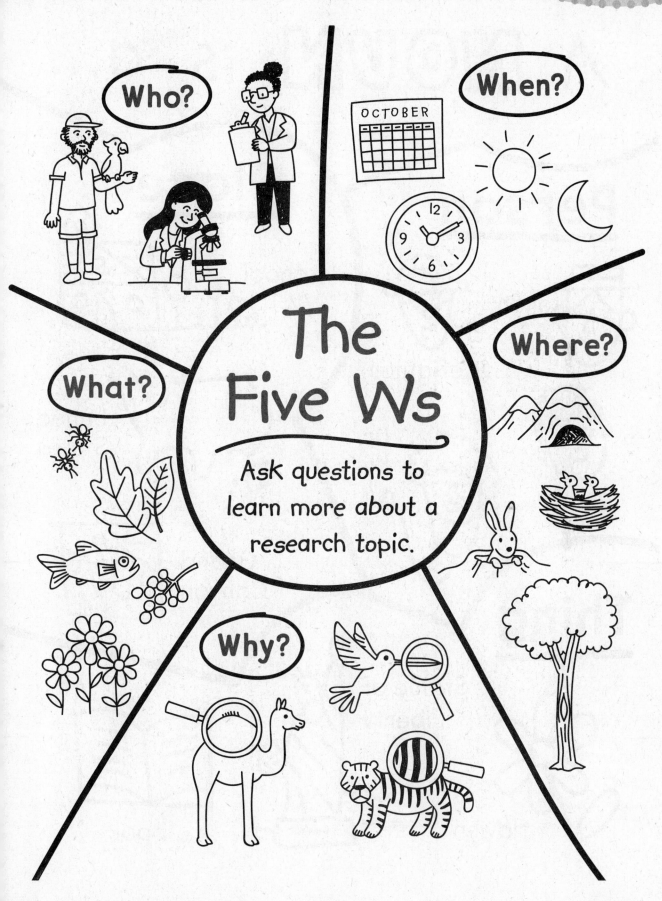

Name _____

A NOUN is a...

Person

 man

 firefighter

 Javier

Dr. Kelly

Place

 school

 United States

Grand Canyon

Thing

 flower

Statue of Liberty

book

Name _____

Verbs

A **verb** is an **action word**.

I <u>walk</u>.

She <u>reads</u>.

It <u>jumps</u>.

They <u>walk</u>.

We <u>read</u>.

They <u>jump</u>.

<u>Verbs</u> can tell the **actions** of more than one person or thing.

Name _____

Adjectives

An **adjective** can describe **color**.

red

yellow

blue

An **adjective** can describe **size**.

tall

huge

tiny

Name _____

Adjectives

An **adjective** can describe **shape**.

round   flat   curly

An **adjective** can describe **number**.

one   third second first   many

Name _____

Sentences

A <u>sentence</u> is a complete thought.

Start with an uppercase letter.

The dogs ran in the park.

End with an end mark.

Name _____

ABCDEFGHIJKLMN

the word "I"

I like to eat bananas.

names of people, animals, and places

Victoria   Spot   Texas

Uppercase Letters

Which words start with an uppercase letter?

the first word in a sentence

The dog is brown.

days of the week and months of the year

Today is Wednesday, September 9.

OPQRSTUVWXYZ

Name _____

End Marks

An end mark is like a (STOP) sign at the end of a <u>sentence</u>.

This is a polar bear.

Did you know polar bears can swim?

Some polar bears weigh more than 1,000 pounds!